Special thanks to;

Laura Cunliffe

And

Kelsey McCallum

Care has been taken to ensure that proper credit is given to all referenced materials in this manual; however, the author welcomes any information to rectify potential errors.

If you have obtained this manual outside of a group setting and are interested in the conjoint facilitator's manual, you may view and purchase multiple copies at www.xlibris.com by searching for *Happiness 101: A how-to guide in positive psychology for people who are depressed, languishing, or flourishing. The Facilitator's Manual.*

To order additional copies of this book, contact:
Xlibris
844-714-8691
www.Xlibris.com
Orders@Xlibris.com

ISBN: Softcover   978-1-4415-8874-6
             EBook   978-1-6698-4866-0

Print information available on the last page

Rev. date: 09/22/2022

Introduction

Welcome to the group! This program and manual is for individuals who want more happiness in life. It is a psycho-educational group offering discussion and individual homework exercises. It provides information with which to implement strategic changes to your happiness levels. Feel free to take notes within the book. The more you think about the concepts and practice them, the better positioned you will be to enjoy and generate positive experiences. This book is to be used in a group run by a qualified group leader who has an understanding of positive psychology. A facilitator's manual is available for this purpose.

Your facilitator will take you through the various sessions. At the back of this book, there are study questions that you can answer, or use as discussion questions within this group, or with your own circle of friends and family. I encourage you to think about and discuss the ideas in the manual. There is also an extensive reference list. The books are all available in libraries and bookstores and make for good reading. There is also a definitions list at the back and many interventions for you to try, but your group facilitator will have many more for you.

Program objectives

By completing this program, you will understand that long-term sustainable happiness takes deliberate effort and personal commitment. Happiness is a state of mind that must be chosen and reinforced with action. You will learn to use many concepts to your advantage.

"Happiness depends upon ourselves." – Aristotle

Why this program is important

The costs of being unhappy are no longer affordable. As it is, depression is the fourth largest disease burden in the world (Hyman, Chisholm, Kessler, Patel, & Whiteford, 2006), and costs relating to health care, lost employment, disability, family strain, related health conditions, addictions, etc, are high. In fact, major depression is set to become the largest contributor to disease burden in high income nations by 2030 (Mathers & Loncar, 2006). Depression is also the most costly disease in the world to treat (World Health Organization, 2008). Because of the stigma associated with obtaining help for what is considered a mental disorder, a new approach to providing services is needed as many individuals do not access help at all. In fact, only about half the individuals who need assistance receive it (Cheung & Dewa, 2007; Rhodes, Bethel, & Bondy, 2006). Yet, it seems that the more we focus on depression, the greater its persistence. What would happen if we focused on happiness instead?

While we are programmed to seek happiness (Layard, 2006), we do not always know how to make happiness happen, and often hold incorrect ideas about what makes us happy (Loewenstein & Schkade, 1999). That is why this group was developed. I hope you can learn what makes you happy, why that is the case, and how you can maintain that state of mind over time.

A note on terminology

"Happiness" as a term does not really mean anything. Seligman (2002) considers it a clumsy concept, and instead, uses various theoretical components. Happiness refers to what positive psychology strives for, and uses the terms well-being, vitality, thriving, flourishing, life satisfaction, and other positive emotions and positive states interchangeably. Happiness does not only belong to one theory either. For instance, the PERMA model of well-being (Seligman, 2011), is one of many which we will review. Finally, throughout the manual, you should know that the word "affect" refers to emotions, or feelings.

A special note on depression, therapy, and suicide.

This group had originally been designed for people who struggled with depression, and many asked the obvious question, "Why don't we talk about depression?" The answer is simple: there is little to gain from doing so. There used to be a belief in psychology that if we removed the symptoms of depression, people would be happy. But, this is not so. If we remove the symptoms of depression, it just means you're not depressed. It doesn't mean you're necessarily happy. The feeling of being in neutral, or just going through the motions is called languishing (Keyes, 2005), and it is an important state to which we should attend because people who are languishing have very high odds of becoming depressed over time (Keyes, Dhingra, & Simoes, 2010).

Let's use an analogy. Imagine a thermometer. Depression is when you are in the minus temperatures. Not being depressed, or languishing is still only in the zero area, and happiness, or flourishing (Keyes, 2005) is in the positives. This group moves people past the negative and neutral zone. Traditional psychology focuses on moving people away from negatives, while positive psychology moves people into the positives. This group does not concern itself with what is found in the lower temperatures. People who are depressed already know how it feels. Consequently, there is a lot to gain from learning the skills necessary to generate a state of happiness. People want to feel happier, and not just "not depressed." Thus, this group is for people who are depressed, languishing, or already flourishing and want to feel better and do more with their lives.

Henry (2006) noticed that individuals reported success in feeling happier by quieting the mind, accepting reality and moving forwards, participating in physical activity, being absorbed in activity, finding emotional support, and developing meaning in life. What people considered unhelpful was the advice given by psychologists (like me!), such as reading and talking about a problem, and analyzing and planning, suggesting that perhaps science overlooks the insight and perspectives of regular people. This is not to say that psychologists do not know what they are talking about, but sometimes, simple solutions are better than complex ones. It also suggests that you are an expert on your life and you can achieve the right solutions with the proper tools and information.

As you move through the program, you will notice that some days are great and some are not. You won't (and shouldn't) be happy all of the time. Despite our best efforts, sometimes we can let our minds get the best of us. This happens to all of us, so don't get too concerned if it happens to you. Just notice your mood and keep moving towards your goal.

If you experience thoughts of suicide, or thoughts about wanting to hurt yourself, or someone else, please share this with your group leader! While this course focuses on happiness, it does not mean that negative feelings should be ignored. Please, do not suffer alone with negative feelings. Talk with the group leader after the session and let them know how you feel. They will listen and help. If you happen to have obtained this book without attending the group sessions and need assistance or someone to speak with, call your nearest hospital and ask them to put you through to the hospital social worker who can either help you directly or assist you in finding the right resource. You can also contact a local crisis line, counseling centre, community service centre, church, etc. Keep telling someone how you feel until you get the right help. If you feel suicidal, you may need more help than what this group can offer you at present. Please seek out additional supports immediately. You can always join us later. We would be most happy to see you again.

Instruction – Activity 1

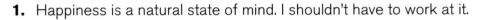

Read and answer the questions that address popular myths and beliefs about happiness. In minutes, your instructor will give you more information about each myth or belief.

Myths and Beliefs about Happiness

1. Happiness is a natural state of mind. I shouldn't have to work at it.

   What are your beliefs about happiness?

2. There is little for me to be happy about; I don't own my home, I have debt, I have to lose 30 pounds, and I just got divorced.

   Is it possible for you to be happy when nothing seems to be working out?

3. Once I obtain A, B, and C, then I can be happy.

   What are reasons you have given yourself to not be happy? What is it you feel you need to do, or have before you can allow yourself some joy?

4. Happy people laugh, smile, and giggle, and can be naive and unrealistic.

Do you feel that happiness looks a certain way? Like what?

5. I have to be in therapy and deal with my issues before I can be happy.

Do you believe you must address painful past events before you can be happy?

6. I can't be happy because I... don't have a good job, my kid has ADHD, my back hurts, my spouse is depressed, or I hate my boss.

How is your situation so different from others? What are some good things in your life?

7. If I just complete this group and do all of the homework, I'll never have to work at happiness again.

Do you agree or disagree with this statement and why?

8. I can do whatever I like if my goal is to be happy.

Do you think that achieving a personal goal of happiness means people can disregard others rights and feelings? Do you think achieving happiness means you can do what you like if it makes you happy now?

9. Winning the lottery would make all the difference to my happiness.

We all say that money doesn't buy happiness, but are you convinced of this?

Instruction – Activity 2

1. Why should you be happy?

Lyubomirsky, King, and Diener (2005) reviewed 225 studies of over 275,000 people and showed that while there was validity to the idea that resources led to increased happiness, there was more evidence showing that happiness invited greater individual success. Positive affect led individuals to act, think, and feel in ways that made success and goal achievement more likely. Positive emotions led to success in employment, job satisfaction, community involvement, relationships, and mental and physical health. Happy individuals earned more money than less happy people. They were more active, cooperative, better liked by others, and more pro-socially engaged. They had better health behaviors and stronger immunities, and problem-solved with more creativity and flexibility.

Could happy people be successful simply because they have more resources in the first place? Some results may be due to the effects of lucky circumstances, but the research clearly states that happiness comes before success.

The benefits happy people obtain also come from the perceptions that others have of them and the resources they gain from being happy. They are more successful in health, income, employment, and relationships because of what they do, and because of the right people and situations they attract.

2. If you were happier, how do you think it would make a difference to your health, family, friends, and job?

Lyubomirsky, Sheldon, and Schkade (2005) consider happiness to come from three points; our genetic set point, circumstances, and personal choices. Genetics explains, for example, the difference between the cheerful optimist, and the persistent grouch. This does not mean that change is useless, but that even when genetically set, we can ensure our positive affect is at the highest end of the set range rather than at the lowest end.

Personal circumstances, such as marital or financial status, account for no more than 10% of happiness leaving a lot of room for purposeful changes. These intentional changes refer to the things over which we have control, such as our relationships, activities, thoughts, and perceptions. Circumstances are difficult to change and due to adaptation (the fact that we get used to change), modifying things like financial status, number of children, or weight make little lasting change to happiness as the new change becomes the norm.

3. What will the people in your life notice about you when you are happier?

4. See the pie chart below. What percentage of happiness do you think comes from genetics, circumstances, and personal choices? Write your estimate on the chart.

The **hedonic treadmill** is a term used by Brickman, Coates, and Janoff-Bulman (1978) that refers to the attempts we make to repeatedly generate positive feelings. When a level of happiness or fulfillment is reached, the new level becomes the standard to maintain. Because the bar is raised as soon as it is reached, the treadmill effect occurs. For example if you make $40,000 a year and suddenly get a raise of $5,000, you will be happy about the raise. But, after a few weeks, the effect of happiness due to the raise wears off and now $45,000 is normal and no longer special. What's more, most people would simply find ways to spend the extra $5,000 and look towards the next raise, not enjoying the one they just received. In short, the hedonic treadmill explains why the more we have, the more we want, and why we are not satisfied with what we have.

Consider Jenny. She is 16 years old and has been working part-time for months. She finally saved up enough money to buy herself an iPod, but when she got to school, she realized that the model she had was outdated and a new one was already on the market! Rather than enjoy her music anyways, her new iPod sits in a drawer unused because it does not compare to the new one her friends have.

Seek to be happy with what you have rather than be unhappy with what you do not have.

Hedonic treadmill:

- Trying to achieve positive feelings by doing things over and over again with diminishing returns

- Depending on external markers of success instead of relying on one's own marker of success

---

Adaptation (Lyubomirsky, 2011) is another useful concept in explaining why good things seem to lose their excitement over time. This term simply means that we get used to things. The good news is that we adapt to negative events too. When faced with tough situations, we generally return to our usual mood over time and get used to the situation. The bad news is that we need a constant stream of positive experiences that differ enough from one another so that we don't get used to positive events and fail to appreciate them. In the case of positive affect, adaptation acts as a barrier to the effects of happiness and minimizes its impact. In fact, there is evidence suggesting that adaptation takes place more quickly in response to positive experiences than negative ones, thus effort and purposeful interventions are required to overcome habituation or adaptation (Lyubomirsky, 2009a). In response, individuals engage in the hedonic treadmill and try to attain the same feelings by repeating the same behaviors but find that they garner less powerful effects than those found the first time they engaged in the activity. For instance, Anne enjoys meeting her friends for drinks every Friday after work but is now accustomed to the scene and is bored. To compensate, she invites her friends for drinks on Saturday as well hoping things will be different but generates even worse results. Thus, by aiming for short-term gains to achieve the same pleasures, individuals find that the standard against which they measure their happiness has changed, or is less meaningful.

Sustainable Happiness Model
(Lyubomirsky, Sheldon & Schkade, 2005)

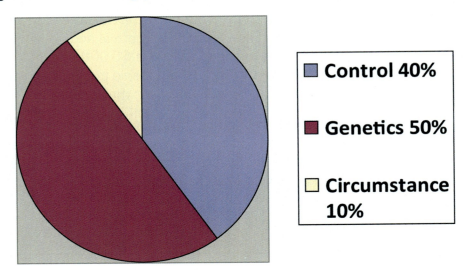

The sustainable happiness model (Lyubomirsky, Sheldon, & Schkade, 2005)

Let's look more closely at the components of happiness as they are explained in the **Sustainable Happiness Model** (Lyubomirsky, Sheldon, & Schkade, 2005). As noted, even when faced with tough situations, we generally return to our usual level of emotion or mood. That is, after any positive or negative event, things eventually go back to normal without much effort. This return to normal is called our **set point**. We tend to return to the way we usually are unless we make an effort to do otherwise. Headey (2008) argues that our set point can change. By setting and achieving life goals, changes to set points occur and result in permanent changes to well-being. If these gains are maintained for long enough, the new level of achievement becomes the new set point (Sheldon & Houser-Marko, 2001).

How can we make sure that we do not adapt to positive life changes?

Because of hedonic adaptation (Frederick & Loewenstein, 1999), the tendency for happiness levels to return to one's baseline or normal range after experience, activity must vary. At the same time, habits must develop. Regular initiation of activity in the same way each time forms habits and reduces the hurdle of getting starting (Lyubomirsky, Sheldon, & Schkade, 2005).

Interventions work when individuals act purposely, and use effort (Sheldon & Lyubomirsky, 2006a) as this counteracts habituation and boredom. The activity must be regularly done (Sheldon & Lyubomirsky, 2006b), freely chosen (Csikszentmihalyi & Hunter, 2003), and naturally motivating such that needs for personal growth are met instead of unnecessary needs like fame, money, or image (Ryan & Deci, 2000).

Further, effort is vital and should be used to identify challenge, go towards it, and use skills to manage it. Pursuing gratification can sometimes be unpleasant and not accompanied by positive emotions at all (Seligman, Parks, & Steen, 2005). While modern life is comfortable and distracting, it often does not lead to challenge great enough to upset the balance between skill and the demands necessary for personal growth (Rathunde & Csikszentmihalyi, 2006).

Commitment is also necessary for success. The more progressively successful one is in attaining goals the more well-being improves. Being in a situation that is more challenging than usual and where skills are stretched and successfully used contributes to success and to the development of flow (described later) (Csikszentmihalyi & Hunter, 2003). Finally, social support also helps individuals initiate and maintain happiness as interacting with peers raises overall happiness in activities.

While practicing these strategies, it is important to remember that happiness depends on variety, and mixing up the activities you choose to do. This will ensure you do not adapt to the activity and it becomes a chore. Effort is important. Working hard at a task ensures that you are focused and appreciate the outcomes. Be aware of timing too. Doing the same thing all the time renders it less pleasant over time. Chocolate cake might be your favorite food, but you would still get tired of eating it every day. Therefore, space out the things you like doing, or find ways to make them different each time so they seem new.

To enjoy and savor, save what you like to do and time it well so that the risks of adapting to the positive feelings decrease. Lastly, while performing a task that you find enjoyable and that brings pleasure, be mindful of your actions. Do not allow yourself to mechanically move through the activity, or simply go through the motions. This is pointless and brings no joy.

Mean what you do, do what you like, and if you must do things you do not like (as we all do), seek to make it better by focusing on things that are not too bad, or find ways to make it fun. Do not just do things to check them off your list. I listen to interesting documentaries on my iPod while I clean the house. It makes it more tolerable and I look forward to doing chores more than I used to.

Whatever your activity, use the criteria below to ensure that your activity remains effective (Lyubomirsky, 2009b).

Effort	Fit	Variety
Skill	Habit	Purpose/Goal

Instruction – Activity 3

Here are some instructions for life that a few of my happy and less happy clients have written over the years. How do your life instructions compare?

Example 1

"Close the drapes, wake up late, go to bed late, eat more, or not at all, watch TV, listen to sad music, move less, stop talking to others, call myself dumb, analyze how I feel and obsess over what I do and what others say."

Example 2

"Seek variety; push myself to do things, put in my best effort, connect with people, walk, lose myself in positive activity, allow myself to laugh, listen to upbeat music, unplug the TV, learn something difficult, talk to myself how I'd like to be spoken to"

What have your life instructions been so far?

What would you like your life instructions to be from now on?

Heroism

Real-life heroes are not those we see in cartoons. Television heroes are portrayed as having magical powers, but in real life, heroes are just average people who take action in extraordinary circumstances. They do not plan it; they simply rise to the occasion. One could say that we are all "heroes-in-waiting" - a term used by Dr. Zimbardo, founder of the Heroic Imagination Project (www.heroicimagination.org). The idea of being a hero is not just for kids. In fact, we can all be heroes and likely already have been.

Think of a time you were a hero and made a difference in someone's life, or your own. What happened; what did you do?

After watching the video clips, what will you do from now on as a bystander?

How can you be more of a hero on daily basis? (Franco & Zimbardo, 2007)

- Remain mindful; notice what is happening around you

- Don't jump to quick conclusions about what you see

- Don't help people who do not want to be helped

- Sometimes helping from a distance is more effective

- Do not rationalize inaction

- You will not always get a good response

- You will not always be right either

You've heard about good deed clubs; what are some ideas you and your friends, or even group members, can develop in this regard? What good deeds will you do?

Instruction – Activity 4

How positive feelings affect our happiness and overall sense of well being is explained by the **Broaden and Build Model** (Fredrickson, 2001, 2006). The broaden concept of this model refers to the ability of positive feelings to expand our capacity to think creatively and keep our attention focused. Better thinking skills emerge in all situations when our positive feelings are at their highest and even more so when people are exploring and engaging in play (Fredrickson & Branigan, 2005). The build concept of this model suggests that positive emotions which develop greater thinking abilities allow resources to be built. Having more skills and resources makes future situations easier to cope with and problems easier to solve. For example, playing, having fun, and laughing with friends after an amusing event, builds social bonds and attachment (Fredrickson, 2004). Experiences of broadening and building trigger upward spirals of growth which are part of developing and sustaining happiness (Fredrickson & Joiner, 2002). Through upward cycles, people become more resilient, creative, knowledgeable, healthy, and socially integrated (Fredrickson, 2002).

When you are happier, how do you act and think differently?

Individuals often overlook many forms of positive emotion because they search for "HAPPINESS." Looking for happiness rather than creating it makes it hard to find because happiness is not a thing. It is better to identify positive emotions and specific positive states so that we can recognize them when they happen. In this way, it becomes apparent that we experience feelings of happiness more than we realized. In the boxes below, write about a time you felt each of these emotions most strongly.

Pleasure/Enjoyment/ Satisfaction/Joy/Contentment 	Pleasure is a sign that an activity, situation, or engagement is of a positive nature (Veenhoven, 2003). Robbins (2006) described joy as a warm feeling welling up and out from one's core that is intense yet soft, and a moment of immersion and fullness independent of any worries. Contentment broadens the desire to savor life events and produces insight by integrating one's view of the self and world (Fredrickson, 2004).
Vitality 	Vitality is the experience of feeling alive and energized and is usually accompanied by good physical health and a sense of purpose and meaning (Ryan & Bernstein, 2004).

Curiosity/Interest 	Interest motivates us to try and do new things, meet others, and explore ideas because we feel there is something we can do, apply, or learn (Kashdan & Silvia, 2009).
Pride 	Pride reflects feelings of self worth and motivates behaviors that sustain positive self concepts and the respect of others (Tracy & Robins, 2007a, 2007b).
Awe/Elevation/Inspiration 	We can be inspired by something or someone, as well as inspired to do something (Thrash & Elliot, 2004). Awe is anything experienced as larger than us; we feel moved and tiny in comparison (Keltner & Haidt, 2003). Elevation invites us to be better people as a result of seeing kind acts performed by others (Haidt, 2000).

Gratitude 	Gratitude is the recognition of one's efforts as well as those of others (McCullough, Emmons, & Tsang, 2002). Gratitude produces a desire to be generous, reciprocate deeds, and attend to social activities (Fredrickson, 2004).
Optimism/Hope 	Optimism helps individuals move forward with life challenges (Peterson, 2000). To hope is to expect with confidence that we can achieve results and concerns the mental pictures of actions required to realize a desired end (Snyder, 2002).

Did you realize that you felt so many positive feelings? These are all examples of happiness.

What are other positive feelings you can think of that you regularly feel?

Instruction – Activity 5

Dr. Seligman (2011) considers happiness achievable through multiple means, or pathways described in his PERMA model.

P: The Pleasant Life (positive emotions)

E: The Engaged Life (engagement and flow)

R: Positive Relationships (family, community, neighbors, etc.)

M: The Meaningful Life (meaning and purpose)

A: Positive Achievements (success and goal attainment)

In these PERMA pathways, there are different levels of focus; one on the big picture and is more philosophical, the other on the here and now and focuses on positive feelings, and the third, on activity and experience. Another involves other people and the last pathway involves our achievements and successes. Individuals tend to favor one over the other, although we can undertake all five pathways at once. The important piece to retain is that there are multiple roads to happiness, meaning there are multiple solutions that can be undertaken all at once, or to different degrees to increase our happiness.

The pleasant life entails positive affect from the past (expressed for example, as contentment, pride, or satisfaction), the present, (pleasure and gratification), and the future (optimism and hope). The pleasant life is one in which small pleasures are indulged like the enjoyment of dark chocolate during a Monday afternoon work break.

A life of engagement involves identifying and using one's character strengths (Park, Peterson, & Seligman, 2004) to be absorbed in activity that provides for experiences of flow (Csikszentmihalyi, 1990). Intense and focused concentration, loss of self-consciousness, and a feeling of personal control characterize the state of flow. Time distortion, anticipation, and the experience of the activity being rewarding are also evident. Engagement is the intensity of activity involvement, interest, and attention that leads to flow. An example of the engaged life is an evening's badminton game where one is actively involved, disconnected from everyday life, attentive, and keeping up with physical demands. Character strengths are the positive traits reflected in thoughts, feelings, and behaviors (Park, Peterson, & Seligman, 2004).

The pathway of positive relationships involves the connections we have to those around us. Relationships involve not only family and partners, but also the connections we have with neighbors, coworkers, social groups, and team mates. Indeed, social support helps individuals initiate and maintain happiness (Boehm & Lyubomirsky, 2009), while interacting with others in a group, generating acts of kindness, charity, cooperation, and support also generates happiness (Lyubomirsky, 2008). Whether for support, fun and play, accountability, competition, or social interaction, relationships of all kinds contribute to our well-being.

The meaningful life emerges from using one's strengths in the service of something perceived to be important, such as valuing and promoting health, belonging to a religious group, or developing meaningful family relationships. The meaningful life considers one's chosen purpose. For example, knitting sweaters for children in shelters because one believes in contributing positively to the less fortunate might be one example of purpose and meaning. Purpose is the reason we give ourselves for the things we do, in what manner, and with whom. It is the why of life that is determined by our assessment of what is valuable.

Finally, the pathway of positive achievements is the last pathway to happiness. Achievements are attained by using our skills, talents, and efforts towards a specific and fixed goal. We put forward efforts to achieve not because we want to win medals or appear superior in comparison to others, but simply because the feeling of achievement in itself is rewarding. The act of winning, achieving, and pursuing mastery does not depend on others. Rather, the standards of excellence we choose are our own. Achievements need not be grand, such as winning an Olympic medal; they can be small personal achievements such as completing a 10 kilometer race or flawlessly playing Twinkle, Twinkle Little Star on the violin.

| PLEASURE | ENGAGEMENT | RELATIONSHIPS | MEANING | ACHIEVEMENT |

To bring more pleasure in my life, I will…..

To be more engaged in my life, I will…

To improve the quality of my relationships, I will....

To bring more meaning to my life, I will…

To achieve in my goals and pursuits, I will....

Instruction – Activity 6

Another pathway to happiness is the healthy life (Fowler, 2009) which involves physical activity and movement. Physical activity has well-known benefits such as positive mood improvement (Reed & Ones, 2006), anxiolytic (Martinsen, 2008), and antidepressant characteristics (Balkin, Tietjen-Smith, Caldwell, & Shen, 2007). The same antidepressant effects of medicine have been shown to emerge after nine weeks of exercise (Weinberg & Gould, 2007). In fact, some doctors prescribe exercise instead of antidepressants (Crone, Smith, & Gough, 2005; Jones, Harris, Waller, & Coggins, 2005). Increasingly, exercise is viewed as a form of medicine.

Through exercise you can meet people, learn new skills, and distract yourself from problems. Exercise can help your circulation, boost energy, and increase flexibility, and range of motion. It also helps with pain control. It can likewise improve your sex life (!) and regenerate brain neurons that are helpful against aging (Ratey, 2008).Through outdoor exercise and participation in sporting teams, you can even see new areas of the city or country. The benefits you gain from exercise can tone your muscles, help you lose weight, and improve your mood and social life making you appear more inviting to others. Exercise can make you more confident, too. Antidepressants pale in comparison.

Kimiecik (2002) suggests that we need to change how we think about exercise. Instead of associating it with weight loss, we must consider the moments of joy, satisfaction, and gratification that can be achieved through movement. Our bodies do not exist solely for functional purposes; they can be a source of pleasure in themselves. Think of how good it feels to stretch, float, race, fly, slide, or throw. Moving the body and experiencing ourselves as fast, powerful, light, quick, energetic, and strong is not possible when sedentary. By moving the body, we also experience the five pathways to happiness. We feel pleasure, and if sufficiently engaged, are rewarded with states of flow. Over time, we also develop a sense of meaning. We meet likeminded people and by setting goals and working hard, we achieve great things and become better versions of ourselves along the way.

If you always feel tired, down, or listless, this is precisely when you should move. When the body is starved for oxygen, movement, and blood flow, it becomes depressed. Much like a car, if you leave the body parked for too long, it will not fulfill its functions like cellular regeneration and the strengthening and repair of important muscles like the heart, or the immune system. If you do not move the body, it cannot provide you with energy, or the desire to want to move. You have a self-generating battery in your body but it must be started frequently. You do not have to run marathons, but, you might like walking, soccer, ping-pong, swimming, or dancing instead.

What will you do to exercise or move more starting this week?

One of the benefits of physical activity is the potential for flow. While flow is normally reported in the context of sports, it can occur in almost any activity. The points below are for sports and exercise, but can be adapted for any activity, like bowling, chess, gardening, working on a motor, braiding hair, baking bread, and fixing appliances.

Flow

Developed by Csikszentmihalyi (1990), flow is the feeling of not thinking but simply doing and being while intensely focused and absorbed in activity. There are nine factors involved in flow: Challenge, Control, Action, Time Transformation, Goals, Intrinsic Reward, Feedback, Concentration, and Loss of Self Consciousness. Your group facilitator will talk about each of these.

Why does it work?

It just feels good. Flow is naturally pleasurable and fulfilling. On its own, it is a major pathway to happiness and is greatly rewarding. To keep ourselves in flow, we necessarily have to improve, get better, faster, and stronger as the balance between skills and challenge must be just right. Flow leads us to be involved in life, to enjoy activities, to have control and to feel a sense of self. Flow keeps us from ruminating about life, chewing over all of the bad stuff repeatedly. Too much free time is a depression trap. Fill up your time with engaging activity. Without clear demands on attention, the mind wanders to personal problems and becomes depressed or anxious. Flow pushes back against this.

How?

Control your attention; what you notice and attend to is your experience. Aim to increase your awareness over the contents of your thoughts and attention as this control improves the quality of your experience. Learn and figure out when you are in flow and do more of it as long as it is good for you. Seek to develop smart leisure, leisure that is challenging, uses your skills, and that is engaging and pleasurable. Relaxing is not the same thing as flow, and watching TV is definitely not flow. Many activities can produce flow, but sport is the most recognized as it has all of the necessary characteristics.

In sport and exercise, the experience of flow is most critical to participants sticking with it or not. Here are ways to create flow out of activity. You cannot call up flow at will, but you can remove obstacles and introduce features to make it more likely. These are good tips for life in general.

- Get moving. Ask questions later. You cannot decide how good something feels until you are doing it. The same applies across life.

- Develop a schedule on your own or with others. Habits are necessary so that the balance of skills and challenge is set. Schedules build rituals; do it the same way each time to get you going.

- Face down failure. You will not succeed every time, but do it anyways. The success is not in the end product. Doing the activity it still builds strengths and resources for the next time you get out there. Bank on building, if not succeeding.

- Move beyond your comfort zone. The only way to get faster is to run faster. The only way to get stronger is to lift more. Comfort and ease are not mindsets for achievement. How to extend your limits? Change your thoughts, or change the environment, i.e., add an incline, imagine an audience, or go faster.

- Believe in your skills. Our thoughts influence physical performance just as much as our performance affects the way we think about ourselves. You must work at your skills so that they are over-practiced and then focus on excellence, performance, and flow. Thinking about every move breaks up flow potential.

- Find the right mix of challenge and skill. You may have to adjust your challenge upwards or downwards and change your skills accordingly. Mentally visualize what is likely to happen and plan for it. Replicate the competition environment in training.

- Forget yourself. This is not the time to think about your clothes, shoe color, or if your hair is nice. Let go of concerns for yourself, and clear mental space for performance. Chatter leads to worry, distraction, poor performance and failure. Let your competitors worry about themselves.

- Accept the environment as a given. If it is raining, then it is raining. Readjust, and move on; your job is the same. Do not carry emotions into performance.

- Focus on the process and not the end. If you do your mini-tasks, the process will lead you to the end without you having to attend to it. Trust the way. Do not get ahead of yourself.

- Have a game plan. Have a goal each and every time. Do not just wander. Be purposeful. Have both outcome and process goals. Aim high but readjust as necessary. Push each goal a little higher than the last.

- Enhance your motivation. Why are you doing this? Be clear; make it intrinsic. Just 'because I like it' can be a good reason.

- Keep negative feedback in its place. Notice your error, adjust, and move on.

- Stay present focused. If you are wandering into the future, or the past, two states that you can do nothing about, come back to the here and now. Do not over-think.

- Do not let what you cannot do interfere with what you can do.

Interventions

1. **Mindfulness**- Mindfulness is the state of being attentive to and aware of what is occurring in the present (Brown & Ryan, 2003; Brown, Ryan, & Creswell, 2007). When mindful, we exhibit an open, unbiased awareness and attention to private experience and action instead of thinking about ourselves consciously, intentionally altering the course of reality, or trapped in mindless habit. Langer (2002) considers mindfulness an adaptive tool in deconstructing cognitive patterns that terminate future options. Mindfulness is associated with more intense and frequent positive affect, less frequent negative affect, and relates to overall well-being (Brown & Ryan, 2003).

What are some areas in your life that you can be more mindful? How will you remind yourself to be here and not in the future or the past? Practice over the course of the week and note how this makes a change in your mood.

2. **Time control**- Time control occurs when individuals intentionally manipulate situations or activity so that time seems longer or shorter (Flaherty, 2003). We can control the perceived duration of an event by slowing down mental processes and attending to the present. We can alter the frequency of an event by showing self-restraint or willingness, as well as change the order and timing of events. How we choose to allocate our time for activity influences how experiences occur and are remembered.

What are areas in your life where you can use time control? Are there things you can do more, less, more quickly, slowly, before, or after? Practice over the course of the week and note how this makes a change in your mood.

3. **Savoring**- Savoring (Bryant & Veroff, 2006) is the ability to focus inwards, appreciate, and augment positive life experiences. Savoring is the process that occurs for example, when grandparents pass the day with their grandchild and will not see him for a time. They focus on how he looks, talks, laughs, and acts, and imprint him to memory. Recollecting memories for later by reminiscing evokes life satisfaction through the positive feelings it brings forth (Bryant, Smart, & King, 2005). Bryant and Veroff (2006) suggest enhancing savoring by absorbing oneself in sights, movement, atmosphere, and the significance of moments, and actively building memories by focusing on details. Savoring is the ability to notice all of the goodness around us that is there, however, we are usually too mentally busy to even notice. Take the time to notice.

Where can you use more savoring skills? How do you do this already? Practice over the course of the week and note how this makes a change in your mood.

4. **Gratitude**- Fredrickson (2004, 2009) notes that gratitude promotes the savoring of positive life experiences given that we have to remember and focus on positive events to be appreciative. Expressing gratitude increases our self-worth and value. Gratitude prevents social comparisons, as we have to focus on ourselves and our situations to be thankful. Gratitude is incompatible with negative emotions and stalls adaptation making situations and feelings seem new. Writing a gratitude letter and making a gratitude visit are effective strategies (Duckworth, Steen, & Seligman, 2005; Seligman, Steen, Park, & Peterson, 2005).

Write a gratitude letter to someone who has had an important impact on your life. If it is possible, write it by hand, deliver it in person, and read it. If you cannot, call the person and read it on the phone, or mail it. Note how you feel writing the letter and how you feel delivering the message.

5. **Writing and thinking about positive experience**- Burton and King (2004) noted that those who wrote about positive events in vivid detail, as opposed to only recollecting facts, or writing about negative or neutral events, showed greater positive mood. Yet, writing to analyze, answer why, or scrutinize aspects of positive experience can sap its pleasure and make us adapt too quickly (Wilson, Centerbar, Kerner, & Gilbert, 2005). Analyzing positive events can evoke negative feelings like worry (e.g., Can I do that again?), or doubt (Did he mean what he said?). Passive thinking (Lyubomirsky, Sousa, & Dickerhoof, 2006), thought without analysis, is better and allows for the savoring and re-experiencing of positive events ensuring that positive affect is maintained. A focus on how an experience feels enhances understanding and provides a way to create new goals.

Which positive experiences do you want to revisit? Remember to only describe the positive moment, such as how it felt, what it looked like, and the sensations you encountered. Do not intellectualize the experience, just allow yourself to feel the moment again.

6. **Best possible self**- (Kurtz & Lyubomirsky, 2008) Imagining our best possible self helps us consider our deepest held goals and envision them achieved. The best possible self prompts us to organize, integrate, and analyze thoughts in ways that thinking alone cannot do. The link between what we envision and how we can make it happen becomes clear. If I am on track to being my best self, my vision fits the bigger picture, and increases my sense of meaning. Even if I am off-track, my motivation is increased as I know where and how to change. The best self provides a feeling of control and direction, and prompts us to engage in active and effective coping. It also promotes goal development and increases positive mood, vitality, and high morale.

Write, draw, or make a collage of your best self in great detail. What would you be doing, and saying differently? How would you present to others differently? Be clear; use lots of detail.

7. **Optimism**- Optimism is about setting expectations of success for one's self. Oettingen and Mayer (2002) clarify that optimism is not wishful thinking, rather, it involves realistic and clear expectations for goal attainment. Optimism leads to stronger performance, which contributes to greater expectations, while wishful thinking produces lower effort, performance, and well-being. Humor, as an attitude, worldview, coping strategy, or behavior (Martin, 2003) is the recognition, enjoyment, and making of incongruity (Ruch, 2004). This form of optimism provides a response that highlights the positives allowing a happier mood to emerge, even if briefly, amidst challenge.

Where and when might you benefit from being more optimistic? Write about it; come up with three optimistic beliefs about the situation or yourself. Is there a way to find humor in your situation?

8. **Self-talk**- Self-talk serves to control thoughts of a wayward nature, manage mood, and increase motivation and effort (Hardy, Hall, & Alexander, 2001). Self-talk can be motivational and regulates task persistence (Gammage, Hardy, & Hall, 2001). Relying on self-talk is functional, but sometimes ignoring it is also good. Successful exercisers, for example, ignored their self talk as a way to protect themselves from justifying, making excuses, or talking themselves out of the activity. In the end, those who used self-talk the least exercised more than those who thought too much (O'Brien-Cousins & Gillis, 2005).

Do you self-talk in a circular fashion and not get anywhere? Or is your self-talk directed, solution-focused, and effective? Consider a recurring form of self-talk which is unproductive; what can you say instead?

9. **Goals**- Goals give us direction, purpose, and control. They also bolster self-esteem and make us feel confident and efficacious, especially as we achieve smaller goals along the way to bigger ones. Goals add structure and meaning to our lives and keep us accountable to our chosen purpose. They help us master time, identify priorities, and develop schedules to improve the quality of our lives. Goals help us cope with trying moments by giving us something to work towards, look forward to and be distracted by, keeping our perspective beyond our troubles. Make goals authentic and rooted in your interests. Choose goals that have a rewarding process as opposed to a rewarding end, and finally, choose goals to approach rather than avoid.

If you do not have any goals, try to set two small ones this week for practice. Consider setting one goal a week to be able to feel a sense of accomplishment. How will these small goals help you attain your life goal? What is your life goal?

10. **Counting blessings & Naming 3 good things**- Naming three good things about events or one's day is a means to find and focus on the positives. As an intervention, stating at least three good things and using one's strengths in a new way kept depressive symptoms away for up to six months (Seligman, Steen, Park, & Peterson, 2005). Identifying one's strengths is a way to more fully appreciate why we do things and how they relate to our interests and choices, thus, leading to more happiness (Miquelon & Vallerand, 2006). Counting blessings re-orients our focus onto the positives, improves mood, speeds coping, and enables faster meaning making. Purposefully looking for the positives when there seems to be none is a useful tool in broadening, building, and achieving upward spirals of growth.

Write down 10 things you are grateful for today. Name 3 good things that happened this week. You might want to use this to start or end the day, or you might even use it with a partner or your kids. It makes for good supper conversation instead of listening to the television.

11. **Social relationships**- We are social animals and not meant to be alone. Social support helps us cope with the bad times and more fully enjoy the good ones. We can experience ourselves through others as they bring out the best in us through friendly competition, motivation, practicing unfamiliar or well-used qualities, and also help us obtain novel ideas. Lyubomirsky (2008) discusses how we do not experience adaptation in relationships, thus investing in others is a wise strategy. We can make time for relationships by making dates of all kinds (romantic, fun, information, exercise, motivation, etc.). Show admiration and gratitude directly to those around you and do things to support others to get it in return.

Who do you need to make a date with more often and when will you do it and what will you do? Who needs to hear and spend time with you?

12. **Avoid over-thinking**- Over-thinking is self-focused rumination, an obsessive inward focus and circular analysis of feelings and situations that result in inaction (Lyubomirsky & Tkach, 2003). Over-thinking results in the maintenance of the very feelings you are trying to reduce. Focusing on sadness, depression, anger, etc., intensifies feelings and makes them thrive in memory (Diener, Colvin, Pavot, & Allman, 1991). Over-thinking makes a habit of negatively biased thinking. Over-thinking impairs our ability to solve problems, reduces our motivation, and interferes with concentration and decision-making. People think they are gaining insight but they are only exhausting mental calories. Over-thinking prevents us from being in the moment. Something good might be happening, but where we are so deep in thought that we miss it. Refocusing to something more realistic or distracting until positive affect is increased and better thoughts emerge can be helpful. Be aware of over-thinking by monitoring its' presence, and then shut it down.

Are you repeating yourself, always talking to yourself about the same events, or going in circles trying to make a decision? Shouting STOP or having a phrase in your head can be helpful – mine is simply – Oh, shut it! and then I go do something. How will you short-circuit your over-thinking?

Definitions

Authentic Happiness: Happiness is generated through positive affect, engagement in activity, and a sense that life is meaningful.

Myth: A false belief held by many people.

Hedonic Adaptation: Events that are initially positive gradually lose their intensity over time. Example: The warm feeling you have after receiving a compliment diminishes after a few hours, or the boyfriend you once cried over for days is no longer the focus of your world.

Sustainable Happiness Model: Happiness is determined by three factors; a genetically determined set point, life circumstances, and intentional activities. A big percentage of your happiness is determined by your own effort and activity.

Genetic Set Point: The point at which one's happiness level is set or fixed, but can change over time. To simplify, this is like your cholesterol level, it is partly genetic, and partly lifestyle oriented. You have a lot of control in changing your diet and exercise, and this is the same with happiness.

Circumstance: Circumstances are the events that make up a person's life, like gender, marital status, education level, etc. These account for only 10% of happiness.

Personal Control: Personal control reflects the actions, activities, and thoughts in which a person chooses to engage. Personal control accounts for 40% of our happiness.

Broaden and Build Theory: This theory states that positive emotions have the ability to broaden momentary thought and action capabilities and build enduring personal resources.

Flow: The feeling of exercising control, being totally lost in the moment, and using skills in a challenging environment that is freely chosen, and reported as enjoyable.

Critical Thinking

The following questions can be done at home. Answer these questions on your own or ask a friend or family member for their thoughts.

1. How have your beliefs changed after exploring the myths about happiness?

2. How does our society view happy people? Example: Not taking them seriously, criticize, respect, or admire them. Give your thoughts.

3. Who do you know that reflects a type of happiness that is acceptable to you (think about friends, family, celebrities, etc.)?

4. What instructions for life have you been following? What instructions for life would you like to follow from now on?

5. What beliefs contributed to your lower levels of happiness in the past?

Additional Interventions

Create a **positivity portfolio** over the next couple of days and weeks. A positivity portfolio (Fredrickson, 2009a, 2009b) is a living document where words, photos, and objects document each positive feeling like awe, gratitude, optimism, hope, pride, inspiration, interest, and love.

For example, a pride portfolio might contain a marathon medal of one's best run, photos, and a journal entry of the event.

A curiosity portfolio might include maps of places you have always wanted to go to, or a copy of a painting that is particularly intriguing. It might have coins you have collected from various places in the world.

An inspiration portfolio might include newspaper clippings of stories about people who have done amazing things, or photos of people who have inspired you. An optimism portfolio might include a letter to yourself about the things you hope to one day see, do, achieve, or be.

A pleasure portfolio might have your favorite recipes in it, a photo of your cat, or child, a tape of your favorite songs, and a small box of chocolates!

Put your portfolios in shoeboxes, label them, make them personal, and pull them out every now and again. You should also rotate the boxes, leaving one out on the coffee table, and changing this box occasionally to focus on another feeling. You can add and remove things over time, so that the box is a constant reminder of your evolving life.

Documenting the Positives

Write or draw about a very good positive experience you have had. Remember where it was, with whom, and how it felt. Describe the temperature, colors, and any details that made it good. Describe the positive feelings you had in detail. Why it occurred is not important, just write about what it was.

Book References

Bryant, F.B., & Veroff, J. (2006). *Savoring: A new model of positive experience*. Mahwah, NJ: Erlbaum.

Csikszentmihalyi, M. (1990). *Flow: The psychology of optimal experience*. New York: Harper & Row.

Fredrickson, B.L. (2009). *Positivity: Groundbreaking research reveals how to embrace the hidden strength of positive emotions, overcome negativity, and thrive*. New York: Crown Books.

Lyubomirsky, S. (2008). *The how of happiness: A scientific approach to getting the life you want*. New York: Penguin Press.

Seligman, M.E.P. (2002). *Authentic happiness: Using the new positive psychology to realize your potential for lasting fulfillment*. New York: Free Press.

Seligman, M.E.P. (2011). *Flourish: A visionary new understanding of happiness and well-being*. New York, NY: Free Press.

Research References

Balkin, R.S., Tietjen-Smith, T., Caldwell, C., & Shen, Y. (2007). The utilization of exercise to decrease depressive symptoms in young adult women. Adultspan Journal, 6(1), 30-35.

Boehm, J., & Lyubomirsky, S. (2009). The promise of sustainable happiness. In C. R. Snyder & S. J. Lopez (Eds.), *Oxford handbook of positive psychology* (2nd ed., pp. 667-677). Oxford, UK: Oxford University Press.

Brickman, P., Coates, D., & Janoff-Bulman, R. (1978). Lottery winners and accident victims: Is happiness relative? *Journal of Personality and Social Psychology, 36*, 917-927.

Brown, K.W., & Ryan, R.M. (2003). The benefits of being present: Mindfulness and its role in psychological well-being. *Journal of Personality and Social Psychology, 84*, 822-848.

Brown, K.W., Ryan, R.M., & Creswell, J.D. (2007). Addressing fundamental questions about mindfulness. *Psychological Inquiry, 18*(4), 272-281.

Bryant, F.B., Smart, C.M., & King, S.P. (2005). Using the past to enhance the present: Boosting happiness through positive reminiscence. *Journal of Happiness Studies, 6*, 227-260.

Burton, C.M., & King, L.A. (2004). The health benefits of writing about intensely positive experiences. *Journal of Research in Personality, 38*, 150-163.

Cheung, A., & Dewa, C. (2007). Mental health service use among adolescents and young adults with major depressive disorder and suicidality. *Canadian Journal of Psychiatry* 52(4), 19-23.

Crone, D., Smith, A., & Gough, B. (2005). 'I feel totally at one, totally alive and totally happy': A psycho-social explanation of the physical activity and mental health relationship. *Health Education Research, 20*(5), 600-611.

Csikszentmihalyi, M., & Hunter, J. (2003). Happiness in everyday life: The use of experience sampling. *Journal of Happiness Studies, 4*, 185-199.

Diener, E., Colvin, C. R., Pavot, W. G., & Allman, A. (1991). The psychic costs of intense positive affect. *Journal of Personality and Social Psychology, 61*, 492–503.

Duckworth, A.L., Steen, T.A., Seligman, M.E.P. (2005). Positive psychology in clinical practice. *Annual Review of Clinical Psychology, 1*, 629-651.

Flaherty, M.G. (2003). Time work: Customizing temporal experience. *Social Psychology Quarterly, 66*(1), 17-33.

Fowler, R. (2009). *Positive health: How to die young as late as possible*. Paper presented at the meeting of the First World Congress on Positive Psychology, Philadelphia, PA.

Franco, Z., & Zimbardo, P. (2007). The banality of heroism. Greater Good, Fall-Winter, 30-35.

Frederick, S., & Loewenstein, G. (1999). Hedonic adaptation. In D. Kahneman, E. Diener, & N. Schwartz (Eds.), *Scientific perspectives on enjoyment, suffering, and well-being* (pp. 302-329). New York: Russell Sage Foundation.

Fredrickson, B.L. (2001). The role of positive emotion in positive psychology: The broaden and build theory of positive emotions. *American Psychologist, 56*(3), 218-226.

Fredrickson, B.L. (2002). Positive emotions. In C.R. Snyder & S.J. Lopez (Eds.), *Handbook of positive psychology* (pp. 120-134). New York, NY: Oxford University Press.

Fredrickson, B.L. (2004). Gratitude, like other positive emotions, broadens and builds. In R. A. Emmons & M. E. McCullogh (Eds.), *The psychology of gratitude* (pp. 145-166). New York: Oxford University Press.

Fredrickson, B.L. (2006). The broaden and build theory of positive emotions. In M. Csikszentmihalyi & I.S. Csikszentmihalyi (Eds.), *A life worth living: Contributions to positive psychology* (pp. 85-103). New York: Oxford University Press.

Fredrickson, B. L. (2009a). *Positivity: The path to flourishing.* Paper presented at the meeting of the First World Congress on Positive Psychology, Philadelphia, PA.

Fredrickson, B. L. (2009b). *Positive interventions: Theory, research, and practice.* Paper presented at the meeting of the First World Congress on Positive Psychology, Philadelphia, PA.

Fredrickson, B.L., & Branigan, C. (2005). Positive emotions broaden the scope of attention and thought-action repertoires. *Cognition and Emotion, 19*, 313-332.

Fredrickson, B.L., & Joiner, T. (2002). Positive emotions trigger upward spirals toward emotional well-being. *Psychological Science, 13*, 172-175.

Gammage, K.L., Hardy, J., & Hall, C.R. (2001). A description of self-talk in exercise. *Psychology of Sport and Exercise, 2*, 233-247.

Haidt, J. (2000, March 7). The positive emotion of elevation. *Prevention & Treatment, 3*, Article 3. Retrieved May 9, 2009, from http://journals.apa.org/pt/prevention/volume3/pre0030003c.html

Hardy, J., Hall, C.R., & Alexander, M.R. (2001). Exploring self-talk and affective states in sport. *Journal of Sports Sciences, 19*, 469-475.

Headey, B. (2008). Life goals matter to happiness: A revision of set-point theory. *Social Indicators Research, 86*, 213-231.

Henry, J. (2006). Strategies for achieving well-being. In M. Csikszentmihalyi & I.S. Csikszentmihalyi (Eds.), *A life worth living: Contributions to positive psychology* (pp. 120-138). New York: Oxford University Press.

Hyman, S., Chisholm, D., Kessler, R., Patel, V., & Whiteford, H. (2006). Mental disorders. In D.T. Jamison, J.G. Breman, A.R. Measham, G. Alleyne, M. Claeson, D.B. Evans, et al. (Eds.), *Disease control priorities in developing countries* (2nd ed., pp. 605-625). Washington, DC: World Bank/Oxford University Press.

Jones, F., Harris, P., Waller, H., & Coggins, A. (2005). Adherence to an exercise prescription scheme: The role of expectations, self-efficacy, stage of change and psychological well-being. *British Journal of Health Psychology, 3*(10), 359-378.

Kashdan, T.B. & Silvia, P. (2009). Curiosity and interest: The benefits of thriving on novelty and challenge. In S.J. Lopez & C.R. Snyder (Eds.), *Oxford handbook of positive psychology* (2nd ed., pp. 367-374). New York, NY: Publisher.

Keltner, D., & Haidt, J. (2003). Approaching awe, a moral, spiritual, and aesthetic emotion. *Cognition and Emotion, 17*(2), 297-314.

Keyes, C. (2005). Mental illness and/or mental health? Investigating axioms of the complete state model of health. *Journal of Consulting and Clinical Psychology, 73*, 539-548. doi:10.1037/0022-006X.73.3.539

Keyes, C.L., Dhingra, S.S. & Simoes, E.J.(2010). Change in level of positive mental health as a predictor of future risk of mental illness. *American Journal of Public Health, 100*(12), 2366-2371.

Keyes, C.L.M., Shmotkin, D., & Ryff, C.D. (2002). Optimizing well-being: The empirical encounter of two traditions. *Journal of Personal and Social Psychology, 82*, 1007-1022.

Kimiecik, J. (2002). *The intrinsic exerciser: Discovering the joy of exercise.* Boston: Houghton Mifflin.

Kurtz, J.L., & Lyubomirsky, S. (2008). Toward a durable happiness. In S.J. Lopez & J.G. Rettew (Eds.), *The positive psychology perspective series* (Vol. 4, pp. 21-36). Westport, CT: Greenwood Publishing Group.

Langer, E. (2002). Well-being: Mindfulness versus positive evaluation. In C.R. Snyder & S.J. Lopez (Eds.), *Handbook of positive psychology* (pp. 214-230). New York, NY: Oxford University Press.

Layard, R. (2006). *Happiness: Lessons from a new science.* Middlesex: Penguin Books.

Loewenstein, G., & Schkade, D. (1999). "Wouldn't it be nice? Predicting future feelings. In D. Kahneman, E. Diener, & N. Schwarz. (Eds.), *Well-being: The foundations of hedonic psychology* (pp. 85-108). New York: Russell Sage Foundation.

Lyubomirsky, S. (2009a). Hedonic adaptation to positive and negative experiences. To appear in S. Folkman (Ed.), *Oxford handbook of stress, health, and coping* (pp.xx). New York: Oxford University Press.

Lyubomirsky, S. (2009b). *Positive Interventions: Theory, Research and Practice.* Paper presented at the First World Congress on Positive Psychology, Philadelphia, Pennsylvania, 18-21 June 2009.

Lyubomirsky, S. (2011). Hedonic adaptation to positive and negative experiences. In S. Folkman (Ed.), *Oxford handbook of stress, health, and coping* (pp. 200-224). New York, NY: Oxford University Press.

Lyubomirsky, S., King, L.A., & Diener, E. (2005). The benefits of frequent positive affect. *Psychological Bulletin, 131*(6), 803-855.

Lyubomirsky, S., Sheldon, K.M., & Schkade, D. (2005). Pursuing happiness: The architecture of sustainable change. *Review of General Psychology, 9*(2), 111-131.

Lyubomirsky, S., Sousa, L., & Dickerhoof, R. (2006). The costs and benefits of writing, talking, and thinking about life's triumphs and defeats. *Journal of Personality and Social Psychology, 90*(4), 692-708.

Lyubomirsky, S., & Tkach, C. (2003). The consequences of dysphoric rumination. In C. Papageorgiou & A. Wells (Eds.), *Rumination: Nature, theory, and treatment of negative thinking in depression* (pp. 21-41). Chichester, England: John Wiley & Sons.

Markus, H., & Nurius, P. (1986). Possible selves. *American Psychologist, 41*, 954-969.

Martin, R. (2003). Sense of humor. In S.J. Lopez & C.R. Snyder (Eds.), *Positive psychological assessment: A handbook of models and measures* (pp. 313-326). Washington, DC: American Psychological Association.

Martinsen, E.G. (2008). Physical activity in the prevention and treatment of anxiety and depression. *Nordic Journal of Psychiatry, 47*, 25-29.

Mathers, C.D., & Loncar, D. (2006). Projections of global mortality and burden of disease from 2002 to 2030. *PLoS Medicine, 3*, e442.

McCullough, M.E., Emmons, R.A., & Tsang, J. (2002). The grateful disposition: A conceptual and empirical topography. *Journal of Personality and Social Psychology, 82*, 112-127.

Miquelon, P., & Vallerand, R.J. (2006). Goal motives, well-being, and physical health: Happiness and self-realization as psychological resources under challenge. *Motivation and Emotion, 30*, 259-272.

O'Brien Cousins, S., & Gillis, M.M. (2005). "Just do it…before you talk yourself out of it": The self-talk of adults thinking about physical activity. *Psychology of Sport and Exercise, 6*, 313-334.

Oettingen, G., & Mayer, D. (2002). The motivating function of thinking about the future: Expectations versus fantasies. *Journal of Personality and Social Psychology, 83*(5), 1198-1212.

Park, N., Peterson, C., & Seligman, M.E.P. (2004). Strengths of character and well-being. *Journal of Social and Clinical Psychology, 23*(5), 603-619.

Peterson, C. (2000). The future of optimism. *American Psychologist, 55*(1), 44-55.

Peterson, C., Park, N., & Seligman, M.E.P. (2005). Orientations to happiness and life satisfaction: The full life versus the empty life. *Journal of Happiness Studies, 6*, 25-41.

Ratey, J.J. (2008). *Spark: The revolutionary new science of exercise and the brain*. New York, NY: Little, Brown and Company.

Rathunde, K., & Csikszentmihalyi, M. (2006). The developing person: An experiential perspective. In W. Damon (Series Ed.), & R.M. Lerner (Vol. Ed.), *Handbook of child psychology: Vol.1. Theoretical models of human development* (pp. 465-515). New York: Wiley.

Reed, J., & Ones, D. (2006) The effect of acute aerobic exercise on positive activated affect: A meta-analysis. *Journal of Psychology of Sport and Exercise, 7,* 477-514.

Rhodes, A.E., Bethell, J., & Bondy, S.J. (2006). Suicidality, depression and mental health service use in Canada. *Canadian Journal of Psychiatry, 51*(1), 35-41.

Robbins, B. D. (2006). An empirical, phenomenological study: Being joyful. In C. T. Fischer (Ed.), *Qualitative research methods for psychologists: Introduction through empirical studies* (pp. 173-211). San Diego, CA: Elsevier Academic Press.

Ruch, W. (2004). Humor: Playfulness. In C. Peterson & M.E.P. Seligman (Eds.), *Character strengths and virtues: A handbook and classification* (pp. 583-598). Oxford: Oxford University Press.

Ryan, R. M. & Bernstein, J. H. (2004). Vitality: Zest, enthusiasm, vigor, energy. In C. Peterson & M.E.P. Seligman (Eds.), *Character strengths and virtues: A handbook and classification* (pp. 273-289). Oxford: Oxford University Press.

Ryan, R.M., & Deci, E. L. (2000). Self-determination theory and the facilitation of intrinsic motivation, social development, and well-being. *American Psychologist, 55*(1), 68-78.

Seligman, M.E.P., Parks, A.C., & Steen, T. (2005). A balanced psychology and a full life. In F. Huppert, B. Keverne & N. Baylis (Eds.), *The science of well-being* (pp. 275-283). Oxford: Oxford University Press.

Seligman, M.E.P., Steen, T.A., Park, N., & Peterson, C. (2005). Positive psychology progress: Empirical validation of interventions. *American Psychologist, 60*(5), 410-421.

Sheldon, K.M., & Houser-Marko, L. (2001). Self-concordance, goal attainment, and the pursuit of happiness: Can there be an upward spiral? *Journal of Personality and Social Psychology, 80*(1), 152-165.

Sheldon, K.M., & Lyubomirsky, S. (2006a). Achieving sustainable gains in happiness: Change your actions, not your circumstances. *Journal of Happiness Studies, 7,* 55-86.

Sheldon, K.M., & Lyubomirsky, S. (2006b). How to increase and sustain positive emotion: The effects of expressing gratitude and visualizing best possible selves. *The Journal of Positive Psychology, 1*(2), 73-82.

Snyder, C. R. (2002). Hope theory: Rainbows of the mind. Psychological Inquiry, 13, 249-275.

Thrash, T.M., & Elliot, A.J. (2004). Inspiration: Core characteristics, component processes, antecedents, and function. *Journal of Personality and Social Psychology, 87*(6), 957-973.

Tracy, J.L., & Robins, R.W. (2007a). The psychological structure of pride: A tale of two facets. *Journal of Personality and Social Psychology, 92,* 506-525.

Tracy, J.L., & Robins, R.W. (2007b). Emerging insights into the nature and function of pride. *Current Directions in Psychological Science, 16*(3), 147-150.

Veenhoven, R. (2003). Hedonism and happiness. *Journal of Happiness Studies, 4,* 437-457.

Weinberg, R.S., & Gould, D. (2007). *Foundations of sport and exercise psychology* (4th edition). Champaign, IL: Human Kinetics.

Wilson, T.D., Centerbar, D.B., Kerner, D.A., & Gilbert, D.T. (2005). The pleasures of uncertainty: Prolonging positive moods in ways people do not anticipate. *Journal of Personality and Social Psychology, 88*(1), 5-21.

World Health Organization. (2008). *Global burden of disease: 2004 (Update 2008)*. Retrieved April 28, 2011 from http://www.who.int/healthinfo/global_burden_disease/GBD_report_2004update_full.pdf